IDENTITY

WHO DO YOU THINK YOU ARE?

EMMANUEL ADESEKO

Identity: Who Do You Think You Are?
Copyright © 2021 Emmanuel Adeseko
ISBN: 978-1-8381796-1-8

Emmanuel Adeseko
www.EmmanuelAdeseko.com

Published by Truthful Taboos
London, England
www.truthfultaboos.com

Unless otherwise stated, all scripture quotations are taken from the New King James Version®. Copyright © 1982 by Thomas Nelson. Used by permission. All rights reserved.

All word definitions are taken from the Oxford Language Dictionary.

First paperback edition May 2021

Book cover design by Kingdom Focused Media

Endorsements

Apostle Emmanuel's communication style offers you the opportunity to heal and establish identity in this heartfelt book. I so enjoyed the complementary perspective of spiritual and practical thought and application. You will feel safe and vulnerable all at the same time, from chapter to chapter. In these days of "Awakening" old trauma must be healed, so that you can be the uncompromised light to awaken others.

Dr. Sharon Stone
Christian International Europe
Prophetic Voice
MyChurch

Apostle Emmanuel is a phenomenal communicator of the gospel and a prolific voice. This amazing book allows us to see how God's voice is present in culture. The issues raised are of importance to everyone, regardless of your state or your estate. The solutions proffered are spiritual, practical and brilliant. It's more than literature, it's a charge to understand and enact our identity in Christ. There is a strength in the words of this book, there is a clarion call for generations that have been mired in trauma and dysfunctional behaviours to wake up to a new reality!

Apostle Tjay Aregbesola
Network Edification Churches

This is the book you need but never knew you needed. At a time when people are questioning who they are because of the things that they have been through or are going through, this timely message will help many come to a place of healing to begin the journey to wholeness. Through Apostle Emmanuel's personal journey, you will be encouraged to know, you are not alone; you'll be awakened to the strategy of the enemy and empowered to overcome, to throw off wrong labels and to put on your true identity in Christ. Imagine you whole! I believe through this book you will take steps from just imagining healing towards the reality of you being whole.

Wonu Adefala
Eleuthera International

Many books written by pastors can talk on the topic of hurt and identity and still not chip the paint work. Seldom does a book come that cuts so deep and surgically combines spirituality with psychology in a way that makes the truths inside not just insightful but more importantly, applicable. I will be honest, each page hurt and healed simultaneously in the way that it took me back to my childhood but also connected me to my adulthood. Thank you for writing this.

Apostle Tobi Arayomi
Founder & Senior Leader
Light London

Apart from being a great friend for many years, Apostle Emmanuel is a terrific teacher of the word. His mastered ability to draw out prophetic patterns from the word of God and how it applies to us today can be seen again through this excellent and encouraging piece of work. This is not just a book to read, it's a manuscript for our generation to clearly learn, internalise and walk in a prophetic and clarion call to our God given identity! This is prerequisite to fulfilling our God given destiny. Read, rehearse, respond & repeat the vital message crafted in this book!

Timothy Adelegan
Senior Pastor
W5 Church

DEDICATION

To my family, dear friends and mentors who have helped me to be all that God has made me to be. I love you and appreciate you all.
To God, thank You, may this book give You glory.

CONTENTS

PREFACE

Identity is one of the most important factors that anyone could ever consider. Your identity is your greatest asset and could be a blessing to you if you know it, or a source of devastation if you don't know it. The job, friends, partner and even location you choose are all influenced by who you think you are. Just as you withdraw money from the bank in order to make a purchase, you must withdraw from your identity 'account' in order to make life choices. Your identity is your life currency.

Thursday 30th April 2020 began with a call from a friend of my father who asked after him as he had not responded to a series of messages she sent. I assured her that I would contact him as he had not responded to my messages either. Towards the end of the call, I received a notification of a message from my cousin urging me of the importance for me to speak with him, so I contacted him. As expected, I received the news...

The loss of my father was definitely a painful and difficult experience. There are no words that could adequately describe it, but in the midst of the cocktail of emotions, there was a flood of questions. Some of these questions were connected to my identity. I've experienced losses over the years but there is nothing like the loss of a parent. We ascribe key parts of our identity to who our parents are and what they taught us. During the early days of the loss of my father, I began to think about these things. I reflected on how short life is and the importance of building my life on the right foundations. This led me back to the topic of identity. It was as if I had to have a face-to-face confrontation with myself in order to overcome the traumatic experience. Although loss is not something anyone 'gets over' there is a way we can overcome it, and any other trauma, in a way that is healthy, as well as being able to be effective in life.

I began to meditate on the topics of trauma and identity and God began to give me revelation which I put on paper. I looked at the material of credible and respected spiritual leaders and the scriptures, which helped affirm the truths God revealed to me during the process of preparing this book.

In all writing, this book took about 3 months in total. Writing the first 5 chapters took place within the month of May 2020. I am confident that it was written by God's inspiration and at yet, through great pain. My prayer is that the principles contained in this book will help you to overcome obstacles and have your identity healed, affirmed, and rooted in Christ.

INTRODUCTION

The Lion King is a 1994 American animated musical drama film produced by Walt Disney Feature Animation and released by Walt Disney Pictures. The Lion King tells the story of Simba (Swahili for lion), a young lion who is to succeed his father, Mufasa, as King of the Pride Lands. However, after Simba's paternal uncle, Scar, murders Mufasa, Simba is manipulated into thinking he is responsible and flees into exile. While in exile, Simba grows up in the company of the carefree outcasts, Timon and Pumbaa. He receives valuable perspective from his childhood friend, Nala, and his shaman, Rafiki, before returning to challenge Scar to end his tyranny and take his place in the Circle of Life as the rightful King.

I watched the movie for the first time when I was a child and it quickly became one of my favourite childhood movies. Who would've thought that a simple children's movie could contain profound and life changing principles about identity within it?

When I grew up and started serving as pastor, God really opened my eyes to the significance of this story.

Fast forward about 20 years later, I was doing counselling training with the church I pastor, and one of the exercises was to ask 'What was your favourite childhood movie? And how do you relate to the characters?' We were put in twos and my partner began to ask me those two questions.

As I reflected on why The Lion King was one of my favourites, again God began to really open my eyes to how relatable Simba's story was to mine. In addition to this, He vividly unveiled how the story relates to the different aspects of the journey of faith and identity for a believer. Although I had used The Lion King as a metaphor to explain the Gospel years before, I had never seen these principles to this extent before. It's amazing how God can use simple stories and metaphors to reveal life changing truth to us. Jesus often taught using parables and metaphors to communicate profound spiritual realities and life changing truths (Mathew 13:34, Mark 4:34). The story of the Lion King is one that explores identity, inheritance, dealing with tragedy/trauma and overcoming challenges.

Have you ever battled with your identity? Have you been through a challenging or traumatic experience? Do you want to overcome life challenges or even grow stronger in your relationship with God? Need healing? Want to fulfil your potential? Maybe you have questions about Jesus? If you answered yes to any of these questions, then continue reading.

Using the allegorical story of The Lion King, I will explain different aspects of the Christian faith as well as share my own story and how I have applied the principles I have learnt.

Each chapter will follow the same format:
- The Lion King Story
- Application to Christianity
- Application in 'My Story'
- Chapter Summary
- Self-Reflection Questions

Prayerfully go through each chapter to get the most out of this book and be intentional with answering the questions at the end of each chapter. I believe that as you read through this book, God will meet with you in a very powerful and personal way. I am agreeing with you that this book will aid in you walking in your God given identity.

Let's pray: 'Father as I read this book, heal, empower and break off any chains in my life; reveal to me who I am so I can fulfil my full potential, in Jesus' name. Amen.'

CHAPTER 1
PRIDE ROCK

IDENTITY, INHERITANCE AND ENEMIES

In the Pride Lands of Africa, a pride of lions rule over the animal kingdom from Pride Rock. King Mufasa's and Queen Sarabi's newborn son, Simba, is presented to the gathering animals by Rafiki, the mandrill: the kingdom's shaman and advisor. Mufasa's younger brother, Scar, covets the throne and is angered by the birth of the new prince. This is the subject of an argument with first Mufasa's major-domo, the hornbill Zazu, then Mufasa himself.

A few years later, Mufasa shows a young Simba the Pride Lands and explains to him the responsibilities of kingship and the "Circle of Life", which connects all living things.

I can relate to Simba. He was a lion, the king of the jungle. He would be the future king in the land and because of his identity, he would be responsible for bringing justice and freedom to the people around him. He was a prince and had an identity that he inherited from his father, but he could not yet walk in it fully because he was not yet mature.

> *'Now I say that the heir, as long as he is a child, does not differ at all from a slave, though he is master of all,'*
> *Galatians 4:1*

Simba is a representation of the believer. We are born into the family of God and are now heirs of God's kingdom. As soon as we put faith in Christ, we have received all that God has for us on the basis of our new identity in Christ. Mufasa symbolises God the Father. He is the King of the Universe and Supreme Authority over all creation. He made mankind to be His offspring and representatives on the earth. Pride Rock is a symbol of the earth or place God has called us to have dominion over (see Genesis 1:26).

Sonship

Simba's relationship with Mufasa was manifested in the context of sonship. Sonship is also the context in which all believers should relate with God also. There are at least four elements of sonship: (1) identity (2) representation (3) expression (4) inheritance. Firstly, with regards to identity, we receive a new identity through faith in Jesus. This new identity is the foundation in which we relate with God from (1 John 3:1). Secondly, the Holy Spirit reproduces the character of Christ in and through us as we grow in relationship with Him (Galatians 5:22). This enables us to be a representative of the Father. Thirdly, we are not only called to reveal Christ's character but also His gifts and power. We have all received unique abilities that God wants us to express in order to fulfil His purpose on the earth. Lastly, as God's children, we have an eternal inheritance which we receive on the basis of being born into His family. Ultimately, when we better understand our identity, we will become more effective in all areas of our lives.

There are 2 major themes that we can see from this chapter:
- Identity
- Inheritance

Identity

Identity can be defined as 'the fact of being who or what a person or thing is' or 'the characteristics determining who or what a person or thing is'. In addition, the Hebrew word for identity is *'pealim'*, which means oneness, sameness and community.

Identity is one of the most important things on earth. Our identity is our greatest asset. We live life, build friendships and feel a sense of uniqueness about who we are, or at least who we *think* we are. The 'Chair Leg' diagram below best explains the different components of our identity:

There are 3 major elements or 'chair legs' that form our identity:
1. **Belonging** - Belonging is to have 'an affinity for a place or situation'. Belonging is a major contributing

factor to our identity. We can draw such a strong sense of our identity from the family, country, friendship group and political affiliation that we belong to. The list is endless. Some gangs respect the concept of belonging to a postcode so much that they are prepared to die for it. Why? Because belonging is an essential component of our identity. We can derive context and meaning to our sense of 'self' based upon the people, places and beliefs we 'belong' to.

2. **Worthiness** - A definition of worthiness is 'the quality of being good enough or being suitable'. Do you feel like you are good enough? The answer to this question affects the very core of our identity. Worthiness is about having a sense of value. This internal sense of value impacts on external factors. For example, your internal feeling of worthiness impacts how much you share your opinion, your ability to make decisions, taking value in your appearance etc. This is also known as your self - esteem: your self-estimation.

3. **Effectiveness** - This is about the ability to function. Our sense of effectiveness can come from the roles we learn in life and our ability to carry out those roles. For example, we are often affirmed in our identity when we feel effective as sons, daughters, men, women, leaders, friends, etc. Effectiveness is defined as 'the degree to which something is successful in producing a desired result, success'. The more effective we feel, the greater our confidence in our identity. Often times, when we achieve these roles or perform these skills, we can gain a sense of approval, which affirms our identity.

Pressure and Security

The diagram of the 3-legged chair above is very helpful in explaining how identity works. If each of the chair legs is firmly connected, when pressure is applied to the chair seat (identity), the chair will be SECURE. On the other hand, if the chair legs are damaged or not well connected, when pressure is applied, the chair seat (identity) will be INSECURE. In this we can understand the roots of a secure and insecure identity. This brings a key principle: who you are under pressure is who you really are.

Often times we may not be aware of insecurities or fractures in our identity until pressure is applied to a particular area. For example, pressure from work, marriage, friendship or even taking steps to start a project starts to expose internal fractures in your security. The place where we first have these vital parts of our identity formed is the family. God uses pressure as an instrument to confirm how secure our identity is. Who you are under pressure is who you really are. This should not make you panic but become aware. The positive aspect of this is that pressure can help identify strong and weak areas in our identity, which can lead to development and recovery.

Image

An image is 'the general impression that a person, organisation, or product presents to the public'. Our image is our interpretation or impression of our identity. In other words, the content and stability of your 'chair leg' will produce an impression of your self-image. However, there are 3 main images a person can ultimately choose to live life from:

1. **Perceived: what you think about you**. This is your interpretation of your identity. It is who you think you are based upon your experiences, exposures, associations and even wounds. Some of the belief statements of a person who lives out of their perceived image may be:
   - 'Well, this is just my personality.'

- 'Something happened in my past and this is just who I am.'
- 'This is just how my culture is, so this is who I am.'

2. **Projected: what you want people to think about you**. Although you may have an impression of your perceived image, you may not be satisfied with this, and or desire for others to see you in a certain way. This can produce a projected image - the way you desire others to see you. Those who live life from a projected image have to make constant effort to project an unauthentic persona. Their projected image may not inherently be negative, however there may be a disconnect between how they see themselves and how they wish others should see them. Some of the belief statements of a person who lives out of their projected image may be:
   - 'People must see me as strong and confident.'
   - 'What will people think about me if I...?'
   - 'My family need to know I'm qualified and intelligent.'

3. **Divine: what God thinks about you**. This is God's original design of who He made you to be. In this image profile, you draw your identity from what He has said about you. The Bible says we were made in God's image and have His attributes (Genesis 1:26). Ultimately both the perceived and projected image are flawed and the most satisfying image we should live out of is God's image. When relating this back to the story of the Lion King, we can see that Simba should have lived out of the image his father gave him, rather than his perceived self-image. Mufasa taught Simba about his identity and inheritance: this should have brought him great security and confidence. Similarly, God has outlined our identity and inheritance through His word and through faith in Jesus Christ. We also must live on this true original

identity, not a perceived or projected one. Some of the belief statements of a person who live out of their divine image may be:
- 'What does God say about me?'
- 'I must be true to myself.'
- 'Even if people may not agree, what does God say?'

Inheritance

Inheritance means 'to come into possession of something as a right'. Inheritance is the fruit of identity. Simba didn't become the heir of Pride Rock because of his performance first, he didn't become prince due to his hard work or efforts (he didn't have any), he simply became the heir due to the identity he had been given from his father. This is the same for the believer; at the point of accepting Jesus as your personal Lord and Saviour, you receive a new identity and become an heir to an inheritance.

> **'And if you are Christ's, then you are Abraham's seed, and heirs according to the promise.'**
> **Galatians 3:29**

When we are in Christ, we automatically become heirs to an inheritance. Identity is the prerequisite for inheritance. However, in order for us to fully obtain our inheritance, there must be the death of the testator (person with a will) and the heir has to reach an age of maturity. Maturity in God's kingdom is not a result of merely time, but obedience and understanding. In addition to maturity, it may be necessary for the heir to fight to obtain their inheritance (see Joshua chapter 1). We will discuss this in later chapters.

MY STORY

Belonging

My family was a key source of my notion of belonging, which made a major contribution to my identity. I was born in Maiduguri in Nigeria but grew up in a fairly small town in England called Northampton. I lived with my two older brothers, my mother and father. My family was a loving one and I always recall my mum and dad working to provide for us. My mother was, and is still, a very kind and loving woman. I remember her working 2-3 jobs to help the family. Mum would literally do anything to make sure we had all we needed. When my dad was alive, he worked long hours and often would come home in the evening after my brothers and I had eaten dinner. He was a stylish man and didn't necessarily communicate emotion and affection. He loved football. I can recount the many times I'd hear or see dad shouting at the TV when Man United (his favourite team) were playing. My two older brothers were simply great. We used to argue and fight at times, as any siblings did, but I could always rely on them and they were my role models when growing up and going to school.

Although I was born in Nigeria, I didn't grow up with knowledge on how to speak, or understand, my native language. I did feel a sense of rejection from some of the Nigerian community because of this. In addition to being one of the few black kids in school, there was some racism in school. This had a negative impact on my identity as it made me feel as if I didn't 'fully' belong to my heritage yet at the same time, I did not belong to the Western English culture. My family were not millionaires, but they were my family and a stable foundation of acceptance to build my identity on.

Worthiness

After some time, unfortunately my parents got divorced. Not having a consistent male figure after the divorce cultivated a desire for affirmation in my identity. My coaches would give me praise and affirmation after every good performance or goal scored. Even with friendships, it was common for people to affirm my identity based upon sexual promiscuity. My masculinity was affirmed by money, clothes and women I slept with. I did not realise it then but there was an inner need/desire to belong. The issue with this was that my sense of worth and value was founded upon my ability to perform. I believed in God from a young age, but I didn't realise what knowing God did to my identity. As confident as I appeared to people, I carried a lot of insecurities because the place I rested my identity on was unstable.

Effectiveness

As I grew up, I grew in confidence in my identity due to the fact that I was a high achiever, athletic and did fairly well in school; my confidence was in my appearance. Looking back, I realise now that my identity was founded upon my performance. When I was 15, I began to pursue a career in professional football, with football, your value is only as good as your last performance. That reasoning literally infiltrated my mentality and ultimately created a sense to view most of my relationships.

Pressure

Initially, I thought salvation meant that you believed in God and you are transformed. However, as I began my journey of faith, there were different points of pressure that revealed the fractures in my identity. Some of these pressures included the pressure to belong, to fit in, not to compromise my faith and to represent God. This impacted my identity because for so long I had been living out of my perceived image—what I thought of myself being a black, Nigerian, British man—and my projected image: how I wanted friends and people to see me. God had to strip away my perceived and projected image so that He could show me who He is and show me who I truly was. Sounds pretty easy and simple, right?

Security

It was at the point of pressure that God was showing me the image I was resting on and my points of security and insecurity. It is crazy how God can even use the pressures to reveal areas in you that He wants to heal. It is equally as crazy that these are the parts that the devil can target in order to sabotage your God-given identity.

CHAPTER 1 SUMMARY

1. Identity is one of the most important concepts on earth. It is our greatest asset that has an impact on all of our decisions and relationships.

2. Though you may have a new identity in Christ, you still need to grow in maturity (Galatians 4:1, 1 Corinthians 13:11, Hebrews 5:14).

3. There are 3 elements of our identity: belonging, worthiness and effectiveness.

4. Pressure reveals the security of our identity. Who we are under pressure is who we really are.

5. Our image is an expression of our identity (Proverbs 23:7, Genesis 1:26).

6. There are 3 images that we can live out from in our daily lives.

7. Through the new identity we have received through Jesus, we connect to an eternal inheritance (Galatians 3:29, 1 John 3:1).

Questions For Study & Reflection

1. Define and describe 3 aspects of identity.

_____

_____

_____

_____

2. Where do you get your sense of worth, belonging and effectiveness from?

_____

_____

_____

_____

3. What does pressure reveal about your identity?

_____

_____

_____

_____

4. Reflect on the image you mainly live out of. Write a list of belief statements that will help you to live from a divine image. E.g. *'God's approval guides my decisions (Galatians 1:10)'.*

_____

_____

_____

_____

5. Memorise Genesis 1:26 and Galatians 3:29.

_____

_____

_____

_____

CHAPTER 2

SCAR FACE

INTRODUCTION TO AN ENEMY

The young Simba innocently confided in his uncle about his future inheritance. He didn't have an awareness of just how infuriated and jealous Scar was of his identity. Scar couldn't challenge Mufasa because he was way too strong, however his plan was to kill Simba before he reached his prime (maturity). This is exactly the same parallel for the believer. Scar can be a metaphor for Satan, the enemy of our soul. He is the enemy of our identity and inheritance. He could never challenge God but launches his attack on God's children; particularly before they reach full maturity. Why? It is simply easier to fight a cub than a Lion. God has called you and every believer to be a lion, however we must recognise that we have a real enemy who will not stop at any cost.

There are two major themes that we will focus on in this chapter:
- The Enemy
- Warfare

The Enemy

'The thief does not come except to steal, and to kill, and to destroy. I have come that they may have life, and that they may have it more abundantly.'
John 10:10

'Be sober, be vigilant; because your adversary the devil walks about like a roaring lion, seeking whom he may devour.'
1 Peter 5:8

'You are of your father the devil, and the desires of your father you want to do. He was a murderer from the beginning, and does not stand in the truth, because there is no truth in him. When he speaks a lie, he speaks from his own resources, for he is a liar and the father of it.'
John 8:44

Satan is the enemy of God and His children. He is the originator of sin and the king over the hosts of fallen angels and evil spirits that carry out his work. His kingdom is one of darkness and his primary mission is to lead mankind to destruction. He is known as 'The Thief' and his aim is not to steal tangible things like our money, but the true treasures such as our peace, love, our sense of worth, belonging and ultimately, our soul. The scriptures above highlight some important truths.

(A)   His Fall
Satan was lifted up in pride over his God-given wisdom, anointing and beauty which resulted in his corruption (Ezekiel 28:17, Proverbs 16:12, 1 Timothy 3:6, James 3:15). He exalted himself and came under condemnation (Isaiah 14:13-14). He was self-deceived and is the original Anti-Christ, first apostate and the one who caused other fallen angels to sin in heaven.

(B)   His Activity
The activity of Satan involves sin, temptation, deception, accusation and death. The devil is the originator of sin. It is important to understand the nature of sin, iniquity and transgression. Sin is the state of rebellion or lawlessness that we inherited as a result of Adam's fall (Romans 5). Iniquity is the twisting of the image of God within man, the corruption of his heart and motives. Transgression is the actions that have resulted from sin and iniquity. Temptation is Satan's strategy to seduce mankind into rebellion (Genesis 3:1-9, Mathew 4:1-13). Deception is

the first weapon Satan used in Eden and is the last weapon he will use in the last days. Lies have the power to shape reality and if believed, can bring a person into mental, spiritual and physical bondage (incarceration). Accusation is when Satan uses facts and/or lies to enforce the bondage of a person. The objective of Satan's activities is the robbery of a person's inheritance.

(C) His Domain
When Adam and Eve were deceived, Satan gained authority to operate over the following:

- The World – This consists of the systems, ideologies and man-made institutions of the earth. The governing force over these kingdoms is the devil.
- The Flesh – The fallen nature of man is under the rulership of Satan. When man submits to the desires of his flesh, he enters into the kingdom of Satan.

Satan and Your Inheritance

The enemy's primary objective is to separate you from God and to steal your inheritance. As mentioned earlier, he does not want to fight with you when you get to maturity, so his strategy is to attack in your infancy. We see two great examples of this in the Old Testament and New Testament. Moses was destined to liberate Israel from the centuries of slavery under the hand of Pharaoh. Pharaoh tried to strategically kill the children aged around two to prevent an uprising (Exodus 2). We see a near parallel example with Jesus, the promised Saviour of the World (Mathew 2). Herod was afraid and tried to kill Him in His youth. Both failed but the strategy was the same: target them in their infancy.

Warfare

Simba was born into a family; he inherited a kingdom, but we must see that he also inherited an enemy and a battle. This is the same for the Christian. We have inherited God's kingdom but also a war that has its origin in heaven.

'And war broke out in heaven: Michael and his angels fought with the dragon; and the dragon and his angels fought, but they did not prevail, nor was a place found for them in heaven any longer.'
Revelations 12:7-8

'Therefore rejoice, O heavens, and you who dwell in them! Woe to the inhabitants of the earth and the sea! For the devil has come down to you, having great wrath, because he knows that he has a short time.'
Revelations 12:12

The definition of warfare is 'engagement in or the activities involved in war or conflict'. As we can see from the scriptures above, the conflict started in heaven and has continued on earth. The earth is a battle ground. In addition to this, the greatest battle ground for war and conflict is our mind. This is the major battle ground in which the enemy attacks to gain territory.

As Christians, we must recognise that we have a real enemy and were born into a real war. We cannot be ignorant! As in any war we must know our weapons (2 Corinthians 10:3-5). This, I will expand on in later chapters.

MY STORY

When I was a new believer, I didn't realise how strategic the devil was in planning my destruction from a young age. Looking back at things like my parent's divorce, the introduction to pornography, the casual relationships and even the events leading up to my dad's passing; I can see that there was an insidious plan that the devil had to enslave my identity.

I was 11 years old and all of my family were away from the house. I remember a pop-up came on the computer, something in me knew it was wrong but the excitement of looking into it triggered my curiosity. I clicked on the image and my mind was blown, there was something about being exposed to those explicit pictures that sparked a curiosity. Little did I know that the devil had a strategic plan behind me being exposed to these things so early on.

When I think of it, there was more. I was also 11 years old when my parents divorced. I can never forget the day I came home from playing football and saw my dad washing the plates while upset. It was explained that they were divorcing and he was moving out. I remember something in my heart was injured by that, but I was unsure of what it was. Although I do not cast any blame whatsoever on my parents, I can see now, how the devil strategically used these difficult experiences to introduce me to his lies.

CHAPTER 2 SUMMARY

1. Satan is the enemy of our identity and inheritance.

2. Satan's activity involves sin, temptation, deception, accusations and death.

3. Deception is a primary strategy the enemy uses. Lies have the power to shape our reality and bring a person into mental, emotional and spiritual bondage.

4. Through Adams and Eve's deception and sin, Satan gained authority to operate in the world and the flesh.

5. The primary objective of Satan is to separate you from God and to steal your inheritance.

6. Satan aims to fight you in your infancy (when you are not fully mature).

7. Although we inherited God's kingdom through faith in Christ, we have also inherited an enemy (Satan). Christians must recognise that we are in a war (Revelations 12:7-8, 2 Corinthians 10:3-6, Ephesians 6:10-18).

Questions For Study & Reflection

1. On an A4 paper, draw a timeline from birth to your present age. Take time to note down positive and negative experiences that took place from birth until now. Put an estimated age and emotion next to each event.

2. How have these events impacted you as an adult?

_____

_____

_____

_____

3. Memorise 1 Peter 5:8.

_____

_____

_____

_____

CHAPTER 3

'RUN SIMBA!' THE LIES SCAR TOLD ME

A PLOT TWIST, TRAUMA AND INTRO TO INFERIORITY

Scar sets a trap for his brother and nephew, luring Simba into a gorge and having the hyenas drive a large herd of wildebeest into a stampede that will trample him. Scar himself does not interfere to save Simba, but instead informs Mufasa of Simba's peril, knowing that the king will rush to save his son. Mufasa saves Simba but ends up hanging perilously from the gorge's edge. Scar refuses to help Mufasa, instead, sending him falling to his death. He then convinces Simba that the tragedy was Simba's own fault and advises him to leave the kingdom and never return. He orders the hyenas to kill the cub, but Simba escapes. Scar tells the pride that both Mufasa and Simba were killed in the stampede and steps forward as the new king, allowing his three hyena minions and the rest of their large pack to live in the Pride Lands.

One moment Simba was a young proud and confident prince, the next minute he was on the run for his life and from his life. What changed? A plot so well crafted by Scar that introduced a whole other identity that Simba very quickly embraced and, because of this identity, he ran. Simba didn't realise that everything that happened was crafted to produce a mentality and behaviour that would limit him from walking in his identity. Simba simply didn't know.

> **'Lest Satan should take advantage of us; for we are not ignorant of his devices.'**
> **2 Corinthians 2:11**

Just as Simba was not aware, many believers are ignorant of the strategies of the devil and the true objective it has for our identity and lives. The scripture above indicates that ignorance is a very dangerous thing. In the previous chapter, I highlighted that we have an enemy who is strategic.

I want to further expand on this by focusing on the following themes:
- Trauma
- Coping Mechanisms

The trauma cycle is shown on the diagram below.

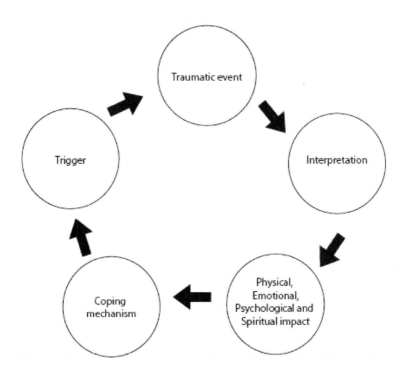

Trauma

Trauma is 'the response to a deeply distressing or disturbing event that overwhelms an individual's ability to cope, causes feelings of helplessness, diminishes their sense of self and their ability to feel the full range of emotions and experiences'.

I have divided trauma into two types - voluntary and involuntary. Voluntary trauma is trauma or intense distress that we experience as a result of our own direct actions. For example, a man deciding to speed on the motorway resulting in a car crash. The car is destroyed and the man experiences the trauma due to an action he is directly responsible for.

With involuntary trauma, the individual experiences it as a result of another person's action or event. For example, a person was driving safely but was hit by another car. The individual experiences deep distress due to the action of another person or an event. Events can also be classed as involuntary trauma due to the fact that no-one is directly responsible, for example, a hurricane or windstorm. Regardless of this, both types can be traumatic.

The death of Mufasa was a traumatic event that Scar strategically planned to gain authority to be king and immobilize Simba in his identity and function. Just as Scar was strategic, Satan also strategically plans or uses trauma as a weapon to manipulate or introduce lies, to damage our identity and hinder us from functioning as God intended.

As mentioned in Chapter 1, the three main elements of our identity are our sense of worthiness, effectiveness and belonging; trauma tends to attack all three.

Interpreting Trauma

A definition of interpretation is 'the action of explaining the meaning of something'. Our identity can affect our interpretation and our interpretation can affect our identity.

The devil knows that trauma can be used to make us, mentally/emotionally, highly suggestible. This is the place where lies are more easily introduced as they go through the open doors caused by traumatic experiences, whether they were our fault or not.

Scar planned and manipulated a traumatic experience for Simba and introduced lies when he was at his most vulnerable point. Simba was emotionally scarred, and this was an opportunity for Scar to groom him with lies. Similarly, Satan instigates traumatic experiences that serve as a platform to penetrate the heart of mankind and introduce lies to bind their identity and ability to function (John 8:44, Genesis 3:1-9).

The Impact or Responses to Trauma

Trauma can have a significant impact on the human anatomy. There are also at least 3 dimensions of fear. In this section we will examine how trauma and fear can operate on the different dimensions of the human anatomy.

(A) Physical

In terms of physiology, the fight-flight-freeze response is our body's natural reaction to danger. It's a type of stress response that helps us react to perceived threats, like an oncoming car or growling dog.

The response instantly causes hormonal and physiological changes. These changes allow you to act quickly so you can protect yourself. It's a survival instinct that God, in His infinite wisdom, built within us when we were created.

The reaction begins in your amygdala, the part of your brain responsible for perceived fear. The amygdala responds by sending signals to the hypothalamus, which stimulates the autonomic nervous system (ANS).

The ANS consists of the sympathetic and parasympathetic nervous systems. The sympathetic nervous system drives the fight-or-flight response, while the parasympathetic nervous system drives freezing. How you react depends on which system dominates the response at the time. In general, when your ANS is stimulated, your body releases adrenaline and cortisol, the stress hormone. These hormones are released very quickly and can affect your heart rate, blood pressure, breathing rate, sight, hearing, sense of touch as well as your perception of pain.

(B) Emotional
Emotions are biological states associated with the nervous system brought on by neurophysiological changes variously associated with thoughts, feelings, behavioural responses, and a degree of pleasure or displeasure. Our emotions are indicators that inform the state of our body, soul and spirit. The pain receptors from our physical body are in the same place as our emotions.

(C) Psychological
While the fight-flight-freeze response causes physiological reactions, it's triggered by a psychological fear.

The fear is conditioned, which means a situation or thing has been associated with negative experiences. This psychological response is initiated at first exposure to the situation and develops over time.

The thing a person is scared of is called a perceived threat, or something you consider to be dangerous. Perceived threats are different for each person.

When someone is faced with a perceived threat, their brain thinks they're in danger. That is because it already considers the situation to be life threatening. As a result, your body automatically reacts with the fight-flight-freeze response—to keep you safe—or a defence/coping mechanism.

The word fear in Greek is 'phobos' which means 'alarm' or 'fright', 'to be afraid exceedingly, fear, terror'. This is where we derive the term phobia. The previous paragraphs explain how a phobia can be created through trauma. It is a perceived threat that the individual has interpreted as life threatening.

Below are some examples of phobias:

- Atychiphobia – Fear of failure
- Thanatophobia – Fear of death
- Nosophobia – Fear of developing a disease
- Arachnophobia – Fear of spiders
- Vehophobia – Fear of driving
- Claustrophobia – Fear of enclosed spaces
- Acrophobia – Fear of heights
- Aerophobia – Fear of flying

The list of things to be afraid of is endless. There may be other different fears a person can have that are associated with negative experiences, for example:

- Fear of intimacy
- Fear of marriage or commitment
- Fear of speaking in public
- Fear of people leaving you
- Fear of not living up to expectations

Although the body may react physiologically as if there is a legitimate threat, it's important for us to question if the perceived threat we are experiencing is really life threatening or legitimate. This is because, although the physiological reaction may be real, the psychological interpretation of the perceived threat may not be entirely accurate. For example, 'Is failure life threatening?' 'Will I die if I speak in public?' or 'Will not living up to people's expectations kill me?'

(D) Spiritual

> **'For God has not given us a spirit of fear, but of power and of love and of a sound mind.'**
> **2 Timothy 1:7**

We must understand that there are at least 3 dimensions of fear. In the physical and psychological section, we have established that there is legitimate fear and perceived fear, however the scripture above explains that fear is also a spirit. In other words, there is a spirit agent that intentionally works to give you a fear-based interpretation of life that results in you being bound and limited in operating. The source of this is invisible and an evil spirit. This spirit is not from God, which confirms its satanic origin. As mentioned earlier, Satan influences our souls through doorways that may be opened through traumatic events in order to bring us into bondage by the spirit of fear (1 John 4:8, Romans 8:15). Ultimately the first time the door was opened to the spirit of fear is when mankind sinned against God (see Genesis 3).

It's also interesting that there are 365 days in a year and in the Word of God, God says 'fear not' 365 times. God does not want us to be afraid or live a life of fear (2 Timothy 1:7). Fear is a great weapon of the enemy and its objective is to cause a person to fight, flight or freeze in their God given identity. This will be explained further in the following chapters.

Coping Mechanisms

Coping mechanisms are the strategies people often use in the face of stress and/or trauma to help manage painful or difficult emotions. Coping mechanisms can help people adjust to stressful events while helping them maintain their emotional well-being.

There are two types of coping mechanisms:

1. Healthy (Get Better)

Healthy coping strategies confront the core roots of trauma in a way that does not cause further damage and removes the symptoms entirely. The person copes and gets better.

Examples include:
- Counselling
- Support network
- Prayer
- Change of diet
- Speaking to trusted people
- Asking for help

2. Unhealthy (Get By)

Unhealthy coping strategies examples include:
- Alcoholism
- Perfectionism
- Pornography and masturbation
- Self-harm
- Workaholics
- Toxic spirituality
- Isolation

The Birth of Addictions

Addiction is a term that means compulsive physiological need for and use of a habit-forming substance (like heroin or nicotine), characterised by tolerance and well-defined physiological symptoms upon withdrawal. It has also been used more broadly to refer to compulsive use of a substance known by the user to bring comfort and relieve them of distress. As we can see from this definition, the individual turns to unhealthy coping strategies to relieve them from the symptoms caused by trauma and thus they learn a way of coping. The individual develops a tolerance for the issue and then seeks more of the substance to maintain the comfort or high. This is how additions are born.

Triggers

A trauma trigger is a psychological stimulus that prompts recall of a previous traumatic experience. The stimulus itself need not be frightening or traumatic and may be only indirectly or superficially reminiscent of an earlier traumatic incident, such as a scent or a piece of clothing.

The Equation

Trauma + Unhealthy Coping Mechanisms + Triggers = Addiction

MY STORY

Trauma

Everyone has a different experience or range of traumas but for me, when I think of traumas, there are definitely a few situations that I found traumatic. The first one being my parent's divorce. I remember coming into the house after playing football and seeing my dad washing the plates while weeping. It was a shock; I cannot remember my dad as someone who was emotional so to see him crying was a big deal. I remember feeling the sadness in that situation and crying with him, or was it for him? I was too young to know the difference. But what I realise now is that children internalise what they observe.

The Impact or Responses to Trauma

(A) Physical
I was not sure how to console him or what to really do. I remember feeling the intensity of my heartbeat and feeling a sense of shock.

(B) Emotional
The emotional impact of my parents separating was strong. I felt a sense of guilt, confusion, sadness and anger. I think being that young but being aware of the situation made me feel like I had to grow up quicker and feel empathy for my parents.

(C) Psychological
Psychologically, I became like an adult-child. What I mean by this is that I had this underlying sense of responsibility for my mother and family, although I was 11. Being aware of the difficulties in my family also caused me to process 'adult' information while I had not yet emotionally matured or developed the ability to learn how to understand and communicate my thoughts and feelings. This made me very good at empathising and listening to other people's thoughts and feelings, but

somewhat 'crippled' me in expressing my own. I wanted to be good, to reduce the stress and pressure on my mum to provide for the family.

Also, as grateful as I was and currently still am, for my mother and brothers, I still psychologically had a need for affirmation in my identity. Having a sense of misguided responsibility for others somehow made me feel that my feelings and thoughts were not as important, which also produced an inferiority/superiority complex. It also developed a need in me to want to help fix things that I may not be responsible for or have the power to change.

At the early stages of my walk, I knew God had a calling for my life, but I was confused as to how God could call me when my identity was fractured. Like Simba, I developed an inferiority complex where I didn't feel good enough although everybody else around me could see my abilities. I procrastinated and avoided accepting God's call for my life; I didn't feel adequate. The scars from my childhood affected my interpretation of how I viewed God as Father and how I viewed myself.

(D) Spiritual

Satan was so strategic. This traumatic experience, the lies, misconceptions and reasonings became a doorway and breeding ground for the spirit of fear, orphan spirit and the spirit of perversion. I could see how the spirit of fear was working and tried to make me afraid of sharing me own feelings. A sense of abandonment came from my father leaving and this provided opportunity for an orphaned spirit to attack my sense of worth, belonging and competence as a man.

Coping Mechanisms

Growing into my teens it was not long before I had been introduced to girls, sports and popularity (friends). I was now at the age where I could find affirmation through women, sports, porn and friends. They became the sources of my security and helped to cope with the parts of my identity that were not secure. The devil used the traumas, divorce and bereavement to introduce lies to me. Because I didn't have affirmations from a father figure, I had to find things to be the basis for my affirmation.

But the devil was using these things to form strongholds in my mind. The devil was using these things to introduce lies that it was about how much money I had, how many times I went to the gym and how well I performed. I realised that not all addictions are obvious, some can be addictions to performance. The reality of it is as I began to grow in my relationship with God, the lies that were introduced to me from a young age began to conflict with my identity, my calling and my destiny.

My exposure to pornography influenced my views of commitment and relationship. Although I am so grateful for my parents, I hadn't seen a man commit to a woman which created phobias around commitment. Also, because most of my relationships were performance-based I didn't really trust that I could be open. I thought if a person knew who I was, they would not want to commit to me.

What was crazy about all of this was that my life was not bad; I had a good upbringing and friends but looking back, I could also see how the spirit of fear was controlling my life.

Just to be clear, I do not in any way disrespect my parents. I love my dad and my mother did an amazing job raising us. My brothers too are awesome! Yet at the same time, the reality of it was that the devil was using these traumas to introduce an inferiority complex, trust issues, destructive coping strategies and avoidance to the destiny God had for me. Satan attacked my interpretations.

CHAPTER 3 SUMMARY

1. We should not be ignorant to the strategies Satan uses to steal our identity and inheritance.

2. One of Satan's strategies to ensure our identity is trauma.

3. There are two-forms of trauma: voluntary and involuntary.

4. Satan attacks our interpretation of trauma.

5. Trauma impacts us in 4 different ways: (1) physically, (2) emotionally, (3) psychologically, (4) spiritually.

6. Coping mechanisms are strategies that people develop and use to manage stress and traumatic events. There are healthy and unhealthy coping mechanisms.

7. Addictions are birthed in the life of the individual when they use unhealthy coping strategies to cope with negative symptoms that were triggered by a traumatic experience.

Questions For Study & Reflection

1. Define trauma and fear in your own words.

2. Reflect on the physical, emotional, psychological and spiritual effects that trauma has had on you. Are the interpretations in your experience legitimate or are they inaccurate?

3. List your current coping strategies for handling pressure or traumatic experiences. Note which ones are healthy or unhealthy.

4. What are your triggers?

_____

_____

_____

_____

5. Memorise 2 Timothy 1:7.

_____

_____

_____

_____

CHAPTER 4

TIMON & PUMBAA: HAKUNA MATATA

FRIENDS, INFERIORITY AND THE FUTURE

Simba collapses in a desert and is surrounded by vultures when he is rescued by Timon and Pumbaa, a meerkat and warthog, who are fellow outcasts.

Simba grows up in the jungle with his two new friends, living a carefree life under the motto "hakuna matata" ("no worries" in Swahili). Now a young adult, Simba rescues Timon and Pumbaa from a hungry lioness, who turns out to be Nala. She and Simba reunite and fall in love, and she urges him to return home, telling him that the Pride Lands have become a drought-stricken wasteland under Scar's reign. Feeling guilty over his father's death, Simba refuses and storms off.

Simba's experience is very relatable. He ran away and was in a low place but amazingly, he had friends that helped him by fighting away his vultures; they became a support network and his new community. Timon, Pumbaa and Nala are a representation of the types of friendships and support networks we can have. Just as Simba's friends and network had an impact on his identity, function and destiny; the friendships and network of a believer has a direct impact on their identity, potential, function and destiny.

Friend is defined as 'a person with whom one has a bond of mutual affection, typically one exclusive of sexual or family relations'. Friendship is one of the most profound, life changing relationships that we have. It is believed that the 5 people we spend most of our time with have a major impact on our prospective decision making and overall drive. Your network is your net worth. Have a look at the scriptures below:

'The righteous should choose his friends carefully, for the way of the wicked leads them astray.'
Proverbs 12:26

'He who walks with wise men will be wise, but the companion of fools will be destroyed.'
Proverbs 13:20

These scriptures highlight some significant principles regarding friendship and association:
1. We can choose - The first principle is the power of choice. Often our friendships can just happen to us if we are not assertive and don't know what characteristics we have and need. You must resolve this truth, that no matter how good or bad your experience is, you can choose. In fact, you must choose.
2. You are influenced by your association - No matter how strong your character is, if you class someone as a friend, they have been given the power to influence your opinion and perception.
3. Your association influences your destination - ultimately if you give another person the power to influence you, it will affect where you are going and how you get there.

In this section I want to focus on 2 themes:
- Types of friendships
- Tips on confrontation

Types of Friends

There are many different friendships but for ease we will separate them into two broad groups:

1. Friends as a result of dysfunction (Timon and Pumbaa)

A dysfunction is defined as 'an abnormality or impairment, or a deviation from accepted social behaviour'. Simba's identity was impaired by his traumatic experience and the lies Scar told him, which lead to him forming friendships with Timon and Pumbaa. This can be the same for any person. Some of the friendships we may have formed would never have happened if we knew who we were. Even if their friendship had some good qualities, some of them have only formed because of shared trauma or as a result of an impairment in our identity and self-perception. Have a look at the scripture below:

> **'Afterward it happened that he loved a woman in the Valley of Sorek, whose name was Delilah.'**
> **Judges 16:4**

Samson was to be a nazirite, this was his God-given identity. As a part of this identity, he was not to cut his hair or to marry outside of his tribe - there were boundaries. Unfortunately, Samson stepped out of his boundaries and therefore met a woman called Delilah in a place called Sorek. Sorek means barren and fruitless, which was ultimately the nature of his relationship with Delilah. He was in the wrong location due to his dysfunction and began a dysfunctional relationship.

Although the verse is not speaking expressly about friendships, we can apply this principle to friendships also. Are your friendships formed because of your negative issues? What would happen if you were 100% in your identity? Would they be able to handle you as a whole person? Or are they not comfortable with the best version of you? Dysfunctional relationships or friendships rely on one or both individuals to maintain dysfunctional aspects of their identity to sustain the connection. For example, a friendship based upon both being insecure, or one of the parties always advising the other.

Traits of a dysfunctional friendship can include:
- Selfish ambition
- Empowered by your dysfunction
- Flatter you but not honest
- Don't protect

2. Friends as a result of identity (Nala)

Nala is a type of friendship that is founded upon identity. Simba, now a young adult, protected Timon and Pumbaa from Nala who was hunting for her family, who are under famine due to Scars corrupt reign. Nala recognises Simba's identity and begins to challenge him based upon it. Simba forgot who he was and was living with an inferiority complex. Nala reminded him of who he really was.

Christians need friends with these characteristics. Do you want friends to remind you of your God-given identity when you forget? Or would you want friends who are comfortable when you are living under your God-given identity? If your answer is no, there is no further need for you to read this book, however if you desire to be that kind of friend or have friends like Nala, below are more characteristics of godly and healthy friendships:
- Positively challenge you
- Protect your identity

- Not intimidated by you and honest
- Support

Practical Tips on Confrontation

In every relationship it is important to have healthy confrontation to protect the connection you have with the other person. Sometimes the connection can be preserved, however if the relationship or friendship is too toxic, you may not be able to preserve it. Regardless, here are some practical steps to help with effective confrontation:

(A) The Event or Issue
Tell the person what happened. This is the best place to start. Be open and honest and refrain from 'beating around the bush'.

(B) The Impact
Tell them how the event or issue made YOU feel. It's better to talk about how you were impacted by the other person's actions rather than being aggressive and talking at them.

(C) The Resolution
What do you expect in future? Tell the person what you prefer to happen in future. This will create resolution and desired outcome if you are to move forward in the relationship/friendship.

MY STORY

Dysfunctional Friends and Relationships

Before I started university, I met a friend called Daniel. Daniel and I were the same age and we shared similar interests and goals. At the time, he seemed like a genuinely nice person in all honesty. As time went on, there were several characteristics that Daniel displayed that made me question our friendship. The first one I noticed was that he would often ask me for support for his business ideas, lending him money and asking for my opinion on other people. Whenever I shared my ideas, life goals or current project I was working on, Daniel would make underhanded and sarcastic comments. He rarely offered ideas and there was an indirect feeling or vibe that I got from Daniel that I was being selfish or proud. In fact, there were a couple of occasions where Daniel would say things like 'you love to boast', 'you like attention', 'you always want to be better than the rest of us'. I was shocked that he said that as I didn't realise that we were competing. However, I was not saying these things to boast.

This baffled me as I thought if we are friends, we should be able to be open and encourage each other, but as time went on, I realised that Daniel was competing with me. The inferiority complex blinded me from the fact that Daniel wasn't really a friend, he was more like a 'frenemy'. A 'frenemy' is an enemy disguised as a friend. If I was more secure in myself at the time, I would have challenged Daniel straight away and I probably would never have befriended him. I met Daniel at a time in my life where I was pretty broken. At the beginning of the friendship, I shared a lot of my challenges and weaknesses. Daniel was always able to listen to me talk about my weaknesses, but I knew this friendship was dysfunctional because it felt like he was threatened when I spoke about my progress. Because of how long we'd known each other, and due to my own insecurities, I questioned myself often. "Emmanuel, you're being extra", "Maybe you do talk too much about your progress". At this point I started to talk less about my goals and dreams. Until one day, while I was reflecting, I thought to myself, 'is this friendship even productive?' The answer was a resounding no.

I realised that Daniel was comfortable with a certain version of me that he had in his mind. Daniel was only comfortable with our friendship to the degree that I wasn't doing as 'good as him'. I moved to university and I noticed that the friendship started to fade, maybe it was because it was no longer convenient for him. Was I upset about it? NOPE! Not all friendships end with a conversation, some just drift apart.

For me, Daniel was an example of how a dysfunctional friendship can be. He was empowered by my insecurities, he was threatened by my progress, he was not very supportive and it just seemed one-sided.

A 'Situationship' With Suzy

Suzy was a very, *very* attractive woman. She was funny, social and really stylish. I met Suzy through friends at a birthday party. We began to speak and for the most part, we got on very well. Suzy liked to party and although she said she was Christian, a lot of her beliefs and values contradicted her faith. In the early stages, I already knew that we were not compatible, but I was curious and found the relationship exciting. It was as if Suzy became a drug (Proverbs 7).

As our friendship progressed, she became bolder in inviting me to house parties. When I began to assimilate a lifestyle that I had no part in, I soon found that both of our boundaries were becoming looser. What started as a friendship, quickly escalated into a 'situationship'.

I knew we shouldn't be together, and I knew I would have to violate or compromise my boundaries to sustain the relationship. The 'situationship' was emotional and sexual and could only continue if I denied my identity. I don't even blame Suzy because I know if I was 100% in my identity the relationship would not have even started. But I received my wake-up call following a pregnancy scare. Conviction started to come to me, and I knew I had to end the relationship, or the relationship would end me. I summoned up the courage to speak to Suzy using the three-step process (event, impact and resolution). In this case the only resolution was to end the relationship. Suzy reluctantly accepted that things had to end. What was crazy about the situation was this: a couple of weeks later, a friend of mine was talking and he mentioned that he had been seeing someone for a week or so. Guess who she was? She was Suzy.

This situation reminds me of the following scriptures:

'With her enticing speech she caused him to yield, with her flattering lips she seduced him. Immediately he went after her, as an ox goes to the slaughter, or as a fool to the correction of the stocks, till an arrow struck his liver. As a bird hastens to the snare, he did not know it would cost his life.'
Proverbs 7:21-23

'Afterward it happened that he loved a woman in the Valley of Sorek, whose name was Delilah.'
Judges 16:4.

The word Sorek means barren or fruitless. This perfectly describes Samson's relationship with Delilah (see Judges 16). When we violate the boundaries and principles that should govern our friendships, we will ultimately end up in a barren or fruitless situation. We have to accept that God puts boundaries in place for our protection. I found that my identity would inform my boundaries. I acknowledged before God and repented of my part in sustaining this dysfunctional relationship. I am grateful that I got out and I'll never have to learn this lesson again!

Godly Friendships

David was one of my first authentic and genuine friends that I had as a Christian. I met David a couple years before I started university. He was a youth leader at the time in his church and one of the few men that were hungry for God in the town that we lived in. We met up one day and I was shocked at how real David was. What was even more strange was that David asked me about my life and my goals and dreams. I hadn't really learned to communicate and had trust issues that came from experiences in my family and dysfunctional friendships like Daniel. What was also strange to me is that David would challenge me to be better; he would ask me about my goals and what I was doing about them. He was also bold enough to correct me when he disagreed with me. What was different about this was that David didn't seem intimidated and seemed to be genuine.

David challenged my prayer life, gave honest and open advice and even sowed into my life when he didn't have anything himself. My communication, confidence and productivity increased as a result of my friendship with David. There were even times when I had forgotten who I was, but David was encouraging. He's been with me at difficult points in my life, times when I've won and times where I've failed. I can truly say he has been unconditional. Me and David have had conflict, but it has only made our friendship stronger. To this day, he is one of my longest standing friends. I don't think I would have been able to grow in my identity without David's support, encouragement, correction and advice. David is an example of a godly friendship where he respected my boundaries and he challenged me to live in my true identity. David also had his own insecurities but didn't allow them to negatively impact our friendship.

CHAPTER 4 SUMMARY

1. Friendships are one of the most profound, life changing relationships that we have.

2. Three key principles for friendships are: (1) we can choose our friends, (2) our friends influence us, (3) our friends affect our destination.

3. There are two types of friends: (1) friendships based on dysfunction (2) friendships based on identity.

4. Confrontation is an important part of relationships.

5. Three practical steps in effective confrontation include talking about: (1) The event (2) The impact (3) The resolution.

Questions For Study & Reflection

1. Define godly and dysfunctional friends.

2. Read Proverbs 17:17; 27:6, 17 and Ecclesiastes 4:9-12. What are the characteristics of a godly friendship?

3. What are the characteristics of a dysfunctional friendship?

4. Reflect on your present friendships/relationships. If you come to the realisation that they are dysfunctional, use the 3-step confrontation tips to address the issue with each individual.

5. Memorise Proverbs 12:26.

CHAPTER 5

REMEMBER WHO YOU ARE!

IDENTITY, MESSENGERS AND DESTINY

Simba soon encounters Rafiki, who tells him that his father Mufasa's spirit lives on in him. Simba is visited by the ghost of Mufasa in the night sky, who tells him that he must take his rightful place as king. Realizing that he can no longer run from his past, Simba decides to return to the Pride Lands.

The messenger and the message were crucial in the recovery and renewal of Simba's identity. Rafiki is a type of prophet, mentor or messenger who brought the word of God that leads to healing, salvation and deliverance. His message and interaction with Simba carries profound realities for believers, the message of the Gospel and the part we play in saving a lost world.

There are several themes we can focus on in this chapter:

1. The Messenger
2. The Message
3. The Encounter

The Messenger

> *'How then shall they call on Him in whom they have not believed? And how shall they believe in Him of whom they have not heard? And how shall they hear without a preacher?'*
> *Romans 10:14*

As mentioned earlier, Rafiki is type of prophet or messenger of the Gospel. If Rafiki did not 'preach' to Simba, it is likely that Simba would have remained 'lost' in a mistaken identity and detached from the inheritance his father gave him. This is also the same in the Gospel of Jesus Christ. If there is nobody to preach the Gospel to those who are lost or fallen away from God, it is very possible that they may stay disconnected from God their Father and forfeit their eternal inheritance and eternal life. Romans 10:14 emphasises 'And how shall they believe in Him of whom they have not heard? And how shall they hear without a preacher?'. This tells us that there is an importance in preaching the Gospel and it is crucial that there is a messenger to preach it. It's a sobering thought that in the world there are many 'Simbas' out there - kings/queens that are living outside of their identity and separated from their Father. It is convicting to know that unless believers speak to them, they could be lost forever.

The word *'euaggelizo'* means 'to announce or declare good news or glad tidings, preaching or good news'. This is where we get the English word evangelist and messenger. The book of Isaiah details Christ as the evangelist (Isaiah 61:1-2). Isaiah prophesied of an anointed 'preacher' who would do the following:
- The Spirit of God is on Him and has anointed Him (Mathew 3:13-16)
- To preach good tidings (The Gospel) to the meek (Luke 11:5)
- To bind up the broken-hearted (John 4)
- To recover sight to the blind (John 9:1-12)
- To proclaim and preach deliverance to captives (Mark 5:1-20).
- To open the prison to them that are bound (1 Peter 3:19-20)
- To set liberty to them that are bruised
- To preach the acceptable year of the Lord (Leviticus 25, Luke 4:18)

Ultimately, Christ is THE Evangelist and THE Messenger sent from God. If He did not speak to us, we would be lost forever. After we have accepted His message, we must also become messengers (Mathew 28:16-18; 2 Timothy 4:5).

The Message Part 1 - 'Your Father Is Alive'

It is a simple but profound message that can change the narrative of someone's life. Simba was living as an orphan. An orphan is someone who no longer has a father. Unfortunately, many people in the world and the church are living like orphans; totally oblivious to the fact that their Heavenly Father is very much alive and present. Orphans tend to live separated or have a 'have my own back' complex. But God has promised that He would never leave us or forsake us. See the scriptures below:

'I will not leave you orphans; I will come to you.'
John 14:6

'For you did not receive the spirit of bondage again to fear, but you received the Spirit of adoption by whom we cry out, "Abba, Father."'
Romans 8:15

The Message Part 2 - 'Look Into The Mirror'

'But we all, with unveiled face, beholding as in a mirror the glory of the Lord, are being transformed into the same image from glory to glory, just as by the Spirit of the Lord.'
2 Corinthians 3:18

After Rafiki declared to Simba that his father was alive, he told him to look into the water. As Simba looked into the still water, he saw his reflection. The water served as a mirror that beheld an image, the image of Simba's father reflecting back to him. Simba was stunned but caught the revelation. He could see his father lived in him. Likewise, when you look into the Word of God, The Holy Spirit reveals Jesus to you. Jesus is the image of God (Colossians 1:15). He is the Living Word (John 1:1). As we look in the written Word, Christ's image is translated into our hearts by the Holy Spirit. The Word of God will revive our spirit and transform our souls.

Remember Who You Are

> *'For if these things are yours and abound, you will be neither barren nor unfruitful in the knowledge of our Lord Jesus Christ. For he who lacks these things is short sighted, even to blindness, and has forgotten that he was cleansed from his old sins.'*
> *2 Peter 1:8-9*

> *'For if anyone is a hearer of the word and not a doer, he is like a man observing his natural face in a mirror; for he observes himself, goes away, and immediately forgets what kind of man he was. But he who looks into the perfect law of liberty and continues in it, and is not a forgetful hearer but a doer of the work, this one will be blessed in what he does.'*
> *James 1:23-25*

The definition of forget is to 'inadvertently neglect to do, bring, or mention something' or 'deliberately cease to think of'. As we have read in previous chapters, the devil is dependent upon your traumas, bad experience and ignorance and pain to make you forget who God is, what He has done and who He has made you to be. God, in His infinite wisdom, has sent messengers and ministries to remind one another daily of who we are and what God has done. The responsibility of Simba's kingship had to be founded upon his authority. Likewise, our identity in

Christ activates the authority to walk in kingship and exercise it over the enemy.

We must be intentional otherwise we will forget or drift away (Hebrews 2:1; 2 Peter 1:10).

Who Died and Left You in Charge?

Mufasa died to save Simba from the corrupt plan of Scar. Although Scar's plan was wicked, Mufasa's death brought a transfer of authority to Simba. Simba, regardless of his age, was now king, he was in charge and charged with the responsibility of being king. Simba's responsibility was reliant upon his identity.

The death of Mufasa is a typology of the Gospel of Jesus Christ. Mufasa died and left Simba in charge. Scar was still in the Pride Lands operating based upon false/usurped authority, but Simba was to confront him through his kingship.

This is the same for the believer. The devil schemed a plan to overthrow God and mankind; Adam and his offspring were at risk of an eternal hell, but Christ Jesus died for our sins to reconcile us to God and impute His identity and authority to us so that we may destroy the work of the devil.

> *'For if by the one man's offense death reigned through the one, much more those who receive abundance of grace and of the gift of righteousness will reign in life through the One, Jesus Christ.'*
> *Romans 5:17*

The Gospel is the greatest news and a great mystery. Webster defines the word 'mystery' as 'something unexplained, unknown or kept secret'. A mystery, however, in the New Testament is not an undiscoverable secret, but a secret undiscoverable by human reasoning, but now revealed by the Holy Spirit. The Gospel of Christ is a mystery to human logic but is revealed to us by the Holy Spirit (Colossians 1:27). This revelation is both an event and progressive. As we read the word of God with humility and an open mind, Christ reveals His identity to us and our identity in Him.

MY STORY

The Messenger

After university, God began to speak to me about my identity and calling and that He wanted me to start a church. The very idea of accepting God's call for my life was both exciting and somewhat terrifying because I knew the responsibility it required. I was conflicted because the things God was calling me to be were conflicting with the fractures in my identity. So, I developed a coping strategy called 'Later'. *"I'll do it later."* Procrastination was a way I coped with some of my feelings of inferiority. Until God began to send my own 'Rafikis' (messengers) to me. My 'Rafikis' came in the form of my uncle and my mentor. My uncle would often challenge my identity and tell me there is more to my life than just my career. He would often speak to me of a greater calling in my life. I'd read the Bible and certain verses would grip my heart. My mentor played a significant role in my life because he always spoke to me based upon who God called me to be and not what I was doing at the time.

I will never forget the time my uncle called me whilst I was completing my master's degree. He told me to submit to the call of God on my life. I remember telling God 'I'll serve You if You can heal these different parts of my identity'. Over the two years of my master's degree, I spent time looking in the mirror (the Bible) through prayer, reading and mentorship. God was able to expose and heal some of the injuries that I had developed through childhood, bad friendships and relationships. I can relate with Simba because I had avoided my calling because of my insecurities, but I realised that Christ died for me and wouldn't leave me as an orphan.

The Message Part 2 - Look In The Mirror

One of the things about orphans is that they live defensively and have to have their own back. They can live life without having a sense of protection and guidance. I allowed my scars, mistakes and experiences to shape my identity and negotiated with my future based on my past. The problem with that is that God's plan for my life is greater than anything I have ever experienced, so my experience can no longer be a reference.

Remember Who You Are

A real turning point for me was reading a book by Reinhard Bonnke on faith, which gripped me because the emphasis was no longer on my inability but on who God is and sonship. I literally felt scales falling from my eyes and restrictions I had built through fear breaking off. I decided in 2017 to accept God's call and plant a church. *"You must be crazy Emmanuel, how are you going to start a church?"*, were the thoughts that came to my mind along with various others. Even though doubts were trying to attack my mind, I knew that God was leading me. It is crazy because obeying God does not come without challenges or the presence of fear, but being courageous to obey Him has such a big reward.

I remember speaking to a few members of my team at the time about the decision and what was crazy was that, as soon as I said and made the decision to follow through, I felt so much power and peace. It was as if the faith-based decisions I was making were reviving and reinforcing my identity. I understood why the enemy wanted me to live in fear; each fear-based decision attacks and enslaves your God-given identity. Obedience is like a weapon of warfare. Although I was in the midst of doubts and questions, taking the risk brought so much freedom because my actions were aligning to my God-given identity.

CHAPTER 5 SUMMARY

1. It is essential that there are messengers to preach The Gospel.

2. Jesus is THE Evangelist. If He did not come to speak to us then we would be lost. If we do not speak to others, then they will be lost.

3. Our Father is alive. We are re-united with our Heavenly Father through faith in Jesus Christ (Romans 8:15). We no longer need to live as orphans.

4. The Word of God is like a mirror. When we read it, Christ's image is translated into our hearts and minds (Genesis 1:26, 2 Corinthians 3:5-6,18).

5. Christ's death has transferred authority to us to stand in our God given authority and overcome the enemy (Luke 10:19-20).

Questions For Study & Reflection

1. Prayerfully reflect on your life. List your passions, dreams and aspirations.

_____

_____

_____

_____

2. Are there any areas in which you have neglected your gifting or calling?

_____

_____

_____

_____

3. Define purpose and calling. Make notes of what you think God's purpose is for you and your life calling.

_____

_____

_____

_____

4. What barriers are blocking your identity?

_____

_____

_____

_____

5. What steps can you take to pursue your identity and
   purpose?

_____

_____

_____

_____

CHAPTER 6

CONFRONTING YOUR SCAR

SPIRITUAL AUTHORITY AND OVERCOMING TRAUMA

Realizing that he can no longer run from his past, Simba decides to return to the Pride Lands. Aided by his friends, Simba sneaks past the hyenas at Pride Rock and confronts Scar, who had just struck Sarabi. Scar taunts Simba over his role in Mufasa's death and backs him to the edge of the rock, where he reveals to him that he murdered Mufasa. Enraged, Simba pins Scar to the ground and forces him to reveal the truth to the rest of the pride. Timon, Pumbaa, Rafiki, Zazu, and the lionesses fend off the hyenas while Scar, attempting to escape, is cornered by Simba at the top of Pride Rock. Scar begs for mercy and attempts to blame the hyenas for his actions; Simba spares his life but orders him to leave the Pride Lands forever. Scar attacks his nephew, but Simba manages to toss him from the top of the rock.

The plan Scar had crafted was insidious, but it ultimately failed. With the help of his friends, Simba awoke from his self-pity, and the delusions that were crafted by his uncle, and was revived to reclaim his inheritance. Simba knew that his knowledge of his identity was key. He couldn't possess the Pride Land without confronting Scar. Scar stood between Simba and his inheritance, however Simba confronted Scar and entered into all that belonged to him. This is the same for the non-believer and the backslidden Christian. For the non-believer, Satan's plan is for you to remain in a state of blindness to your identity and inheritance due to the false narrative that he has given you. Through Christ you can overcome the lies of the devil and enter into a life changing relationship with God through Jesus.

For the backslidden Christian, Satan's plan is for you to stay in a place of slumber and distance from your true identity in Christ.   Regardless of which one you are, Christ's sacrifice on The Cross has the power to break the lies of the devil, restore you and empower you to walk in your God-given inheritance. However, the prerequisite to possession is confrontation like we see when Simba confronts Scar. Will you confront your Scar? Like Simba, the believer must confront the demonic lies that surround the narrative Satan uses to enslave their identity in order to walk in God's full inheritance.

The Importance of Confrontation

The dictionary definition of the word 'confront' is to 'come face to face with (someone) with hostile or argumentative intent'. Hostility sounds aggressive but when we understand the level of hostility that the devil has concerning us, we will be more aggressive in confronting the enemy.
- Moses confronted Pharaoh
- Jehu confronted Jezabel

The focus of this chapter will be how you confront the scars, traumas and lies that have hindered you from being who God has made you to be and doing what God has made you to do.

How to Apply the Cross to Your Identity

The Gospel is the single most life changing message that anyone can hear and experience. Using the diagram and identity in Chapter 1, we will first look at how Christ's sacrifice is applied to our identity.

There are 3 major elements that form our identity:

Belonging

Belonging is to have 'an affinity for a place or situation'. Belonging is such a major contributing factor to our identity. In, 1 Corinthians 3:23 [International Standard Version] it says, '*And you belong to Christ, and Christ belongs to God*'. Through Adam, we belonged to the devil and were his possession. Through Christ we now belong to God. Take a moment to think about that. YOU BELONG TO GOD. This is what The Cross achieved for you - that you no longer need to fear the spiritual, emotional and psychological damage and lies of not belonging anywhere. You do not belong to that addiction; you belong to God. You do not belong to that abusive partner or family member; you belong to God. You do not belong to that failure or mistake; you belong to God. You do not belong to that company or business; you belong to God. You do not belong to that disease; you belong to God. You do not belong to the debt collectors; you belong to God! Christ was rejected so that you could be accepted by the Father (Ephesians 1:6-10, 2:13).

Application: (1) List words that have come to your mind through experience or people that have made you feel as if you do not belong. (2) Use the truth from the scriptures in the section above to confront the negative thoughts and lies through prayer.

Worthiness

A definition of worthiness is 'the quality of being good enough; suitability'. Do you feel like you are good enough? The answer to this question affects the very core of our identity. Worthiness is about having a sense of value, that your opinion is good enough, your voice, decision making is founded upon your sense of worth. This is also known as your self -esteem - your self-estimation.

In Luke 12:7 it says *'But the very hairs of your head are all numbered. Do not fear therefore; you are of more value than many sparrows'*. Even before Christ died, God had revealed the value He sees in us. It is such a shame that one man's trash is actually Christ's treasure! Christ gave a parable likening the Kingdom of God to a man who found a pearl of great price and when it was found, he sold everything to purchase it (see Matthew 13:45-46). We must understand that you are that pearl of great price! God bankrupt heaven to purchase your salvation. The Cross is not only a revelation of God's love and justice but a revelation of your value and worth to God! It is simply a lie and offence to God to say that you are not worth anything when you cost Him His blood!

Application: (1) List words that have come to your mind through experience or people that have made you feel as if you are not worthy. (2) Use the truth from the scriptures in the section above to confront these negative thoughts and lies through prayer.

Effectiveness

Effectiveness is 'the degree to which something is successful in producing a desired result; success'. The more effective we feel, the greater our confidence in our identity. Philippians 4:13 says, 'I can do all things through Christ who strengthens me'. Christ's sacrifice transferred to us the ability to be effective in all aspects of our identity. He gave us the ability to go beyond our ability. This ability is also known as grace. It is the divine ability of God that empowers us to function in all aspects of our lives (Philippians 2:12-13).

Application: (1) List words that have come to your mind through experience or people that have made you feel as if you are not effective. (2) Use the truth from the scriptures in the section above to confront the negative thoughts and lies through prayer.

Foundations of Our Identity in Christ

Our healing, restoration and confidence must be founded upon the next 3 points as they are also the basis of our authority to confront the enemy:

1. The Blood of Christ (Revelations 12:9, Leviticus 17)
The word 'atonement' means 'to be made one', 'to reconcile, to bring about agreement or concord'. Thus, it may read 'at-one-ment'; the making at-one of those that have previously disagreed. It therefore means:
- To cover
- To purge
- To reconcile after enmity or controversy
- To make amends

Man broke God's holy law, which brought him under the power of sin and ensured the penalty of death (Genesis 2:17). In the Old Testament, atonement for man's sins was made through the sacrifices of the blood of bulls and rams to bring temporary forgiveness for sins. The innocence of the animal would be transferred unto the person. Now atonement has been made completely and eternally by Jesus' death on The Cross - His blood has washed our sins, covered us, purged us and reconciled us to God completely and utterly. The blood is the authority in which every and any accusation of Satan is silenced (Revelations 12:9).

2. The Name of Jesus (Acts 4:12, 1 John 5:8, John 1:1, Revelation 19:13)
Faith in the name of Jesus activates the power of atonement for anyone who believes that He died for their sins and rose from the dead. We have access to the Father and receive a new identity as sons of God.

3. The Word of God (Mathew 4, John 1:1, Ephesians 6:12, Hebrew 1:1-3)
The Bible is the Word of God in written from. It is the written revelation of God, His ways and His kingdom. It holds authority to command and instruct us in righteousness (2 Timothy 3:16). Even Jesus and the devil affirm scripture to be the word of God (see Mathew 4). It is the basis for believers to confront positive forces of evil. The scripture is the founder of the believer's authority.

Practical Steps to Overcome Trauma

There are some practical steps that can help a person to confront the traumas that they have faced and overcome them.

1. Find A Safe Place and Safe People
Safe is defined as 'protected from or not exposed to danger or risk; not likely to be harmed or lost'. There are people and places that need to fit this definition in order to be classed as safe. To effectively recover or overcome you will require people and non-hostile environments.

2. Investigate With Help From Your Safe People

With the aid of safe people, it is important to explore those fears, phobia and traumas - what happened and its impact on you. They will help you to see the impacts on you that you may not see. Ultimately, God will help bring clarity as you journey through your experiences with trusted people.

3. Allow Yourself to be Honest

One of the greatest ways to overcome a trauma, or any distressing issue, is to ACKNOWLEDGE first! Be honest about what you are facing without trying to minimise or create excuses for yourself or the other person. Before you can progress, you must be honest with where you currently are.

4. Review Coping Mechanism, Self-Talk and Self-Belief

With the aid of prayer, reflection and safe people; list some of the strategies you have used to cope with your phobias/traumas. At this stage it does not matter whether they are good or bad but it is important to recognise what they are. For example, a coping strategy can be avoiding the conversation when someone asks you about your childhood.

5. Be Patient With Yourself

Transformation is both instant and progressive. We can experience instant change but must respect that some change is progressive. Give yourself permission to go through a process of recovery, which may take days or weeks or months.

6. Set Small Goals and One Focus At A Time

Rather than focusing on doing the impossible, start by focusing on incremental growth in one area. For example, once a week you will focus on overcoming your fear of vulnerability by checking in once a week with your safe people.

7. Re-Discover The Truth Of What God Has Said
In the previous sections relating to worthiness, belonging and effectiveness you were to write a list of beliefs that were negative. For each belief, you need to have a truth found in scripture that counteracts it. For example, 'My dad says I don't belong anywhere' but God's word says 'Though my father and mother forsake me, the Lord will receive me.' (Psalm 27:10).

8. Create New Habits and Self Affirmations
We must understand that phobias and traumas inform habits and even personality to an extent. Start to focus on creating 1-2 new habits over the next 14-21 days. This consistency will solidify the habit.

9. Forgive Yourself and Those Who Hurt You
You will need to forgive yourself and the ones who have harmed you to truly be free from the trauma. This may mean acknowledging and surrendering any anger or frustration that you might have built towards God. For example, some people have blamed God for the abuse that they suffered in childhood.

We Have Authority Through Jesus

'Behold, I give you the authority to trample on serpents and scorpions, and over all the power of the enemy, and nothing shall by any means hurt you.'
Luke 10:19

'And I will give you the keys of the kingdom of heaven, and whatever you bind on earth will be bound in heaven, and whatever you loose on earth will be loosed in heaven.'
Mathew 16:19

As a child of God, you must recognise that Jesus has given you authority over the devil, sin and all the power of the enemy. In Luke 10:19 is says that Jesus has given us 'authority' over all the 'power of the enemy. It's important to note that the words 'authority' and 'power' have different meanings. Authority defined is 'the power or legal right to give orders, make decisions, and enforce obedience'. Whereas power means 'the ability or capacity to do something or act in a particular way'. Jesus has given us legal right to enforce obedience over the devil's power. For example, when a policeman stops a car on the road, this is with authority that has been given to him by his government. He does not stop the car with his physical power and he may in fact not be stronger in ability than the driver, however he has authority. This is the same for Christians. Jesus gave us authority over all the enemy's ability! We have legal right over the enemy's might.

We can express our God given authority through binding and loosing. Peter received the authority to bind and loose after the Father revealed to him that Jesus was the Christ. This is the same for all Christians. We have the authority to bind and loose in the place of prayer.

To bind means 'to make secure by tying, to confine, to restrict with bonds, to contain with legal authority'. God has given us legal authority to bind all attacks of the enemy in our lives. We may need to bind sickness, fear, confusion, depression, witchcraft, and trauma.

To loose means 'to untie, free from restraint, to detach, disconnect, break away, escape, separate, unbind, unchain, to destroy, release, forgive'. Jesus has given us authority to loose people from confusion, depression, insanity, past hurts, rejection and trauma. We are even able to loose ourself from oppression of the enemy in the place of prayer (Isaiah 52:2).

Overcoming Trauma Through Prayer

1. List all the negative words that have affected your sense of (a) worthiness (b) belonging (c) effectiveness.
2. Pray and confess before God how these words have effected your identity.
3. Repent - ask God to forgive you for accepting these words, actions and thoughts in your life.
4. Thank God for Jesus' death on The Cross.
5. Renounce all those words, lies, thoughts and their impact on you through prayer.
6. Declare what God has said over you through His word. Repeat as God leads you by faith and sense God's peace.

Prayer guideline: Father, I commit these thoughts and words that were said by [person's name] or thoughts when [say the experience], into Your hands. I confess that it made me feel rejected and like I do not belong. Father, I thank You that Your Word says [use a scripture], therefore I come out of agreement with these lies in the name of Jesus. I declare them to be void of power over my identity in the name of Jesus! Father, I thank You for what you have said about me and I renounce these words in Jesus' name, amen.

MY STORY

Importance of Confrontation

One of the most difficult confrontations is not coming face-to-face with someone else but coming face-to-face with yourself. Not only did I have to face Satan, my enemy, I had to face the inner me – the lies he told me through my scars. After understanding the power of the cross, I now needed to apply that truth to the different areas of my fractured identity.

Applying the Cross to My Identity

Belonging

The fractures in my identity, that were created through some of my experiences, created an undertone of rejection which led to me having trust issues and holding my relationships lightly because I didn't feel like they were going to last. Why would I give people access if they were not going to be there in the long run? I even got to the point where I didn't think I needed close friends or even mentors because of difficult experiences such as betrayal.

However, when God revealed to me that I belong to Him, it broke the spirit of rejection from my life that was causing me to keep people at arm's length. Knowing that I am accepted by God has helped break the fear of being rejected by people. This has helped me to build closer relationships because I know that my source of belonging comes from God; even if people don't accept me, it does not affect my identity. I realised that you have to be delivered from people in order to love them. Our injuries and feelings of rejection can make us pre-occupied with trying to please or belong to people, but as I said before, ultimately, our source of identity should come from belonging to God.

Worthiness

One of the most profound things that the crucifixion has revealed is our value. When you think about it, if you're going to buy something, you consider the cost of the item and if it is worth paying for. Realising that, not only did Christ pay the price on The Cross for me but He also thinks I'm worth it, which has given me confidence. Think about it, God values you at the price of the blood of His only Son. Sometimes, because we go through traumatic experiences the devil can use that to tell us lies about our value. I've learnt that my worth comes from God's Word and not my wounds or the lies the devil spoke to me through them.

Because of bad friendships and relationship experiences, I would be quite hard on myself and at times, felt unworthy or inadequate. In essence, I had quite negative self-talk. Understanding that God values me has helped me to change my self-talk from negative to positive. I say daily affirmations to myself, which have helped break limiting beliefs and mindsets. The change didn't happen in a day, I needed to be intentional to confront the lies in my mind and build my worth based upon His truth, not the negative experiences.

Effectiveness

As mentioned previously, from an early age, my goal was to play professional football. With football, you are only as good as your last performance. I had taken this mindset into my relationship with God and tried to perform to gain acceptance. When you perform well, in sports, you get approval that builds your self-esteem or identity. In other words, your identity is founded upon your performance. The problem with this is if you stop performing, your approval goes, along with your self-esteem or sense of identity.

You may not be a footballer but many of us apply this same principle in our life and relationship with God. For example, performing could relate to getting the job, the body type, having the money or if it's with God: 'read your bible', fast, evangelise every day. Although these things are not bad in themselves, they cannot be the foundation of your self-esteem or right standing with God. However, with God, Christ performed, and we inherited His approval, self-esteem and His identity. So, my identity now is not founded upon my performance but Christ's performance. Christ's work on the cross makes it so that I don't work *for* righteousness, but I work *from* the place of righteousness. For example, I pray from a place of right standing with God rather than to earn righteousness.

Now, I don't perform to be right with God, Christ has performed to make me right with God. We don't work for righteousness; we work from the place of righteousness.

Practical Steps to Overcome Trauma:

1. A Safe Place and Safe People
I am grateful for the safe people in my life. I will never forget the time I completely off-loaded to my mentor. He was warm, patient and non-judgemental which allowed me to feel safe and honest about the scars in my life. 'Emmanuel, I don't care whether you shout, scream or swear, I just want you to be open', is what he would say. I was surprised. Don't think for a second he was condoning me to use abusive language; he was just assuring me I was in a safe environment where I could open up. And it worked. I began to share with him different parts of my life where I had been wounded or ashamed and he would look at me without any judgement and nod his head; which prompted me to continue. I thought 'he must think I'm crazy,' and the next time we met I tried to share more shocking things to see if he would react, but he never did. He simply listened,

empathised and gave me practical, biblical advice that didn't feel patronising or condescending. This experience taught me the importance of how safety produces trust that can help us to share about our traumas and pursue freedom from them also. A good question to ask is 'how do you find safe people?'.

A few characteristics that will help you identify a safe person are:
- Non-judgmental – they don't condone sin but won't condemn you for it.
- Reliable – they are available and consistent.
- Honest – they'll tell you the truth.
- Assertive – they can challenge you in an appropriate, non-judgmental way.
- Mature – they have good understanding, are emotionally intelligent and can offer practical, biblically-sound advice.

2. Investigate With Help From Safe People
During some of our discussions, he would ask me questions which helped me identify some of the sources of my fears, insecurities and dysfunctional behaviour. It's crazy how just by someone else going through your experiences with you can help to give another perspective and expose lies that keep us bound. A good safe person will not just listen, but they will support you to prayerfully work through your experiences.

3. Allow Yourself to Be Honest
There is a scripture that really helped me with this thing called honesty – Psalms 51:6, 'Behold, You desire truth in the inward parts, and in the hidden part You will make me to know wisdom'. This scripture has taught me that God desires truth (honesty). When I started to become honest about the things that were affecting my identity with God and safe people, I started to see a lot of healing. God can only heal the real you, not who you pretend to be. In the bible, Adam covered his nakedness and shame with fig

leaves (Genesis 3:7) to avoid God. The fig leaves represent our human attempts to hide from God.

When I took away all types of façade and got honest with God, He began to heal the broken areas. It is so important that we don't tell God and trusted people the things we think they want to hear.

4. Review Coping Mechanisms, Self-Talk and Self-Belief

These honest conversations with God and trusted people exposed that the ways I dealt with my injuries were unhealthy. Pornography, women, drinking etc. were used as comfort blankets or 'fig leaves' to cover the fractures. It was difficult to acknowledge how I medicated my issues before, but we didn't stop there. We compared the ways God says that we can cope with the issues in our lives. Here are some healthy coping strategies that I've used personally:

- Prayer
- Counselling
- Exercise
- Friendships and accountability
- Journaling
- Avoiding toxic people or places

5. Be Patient With Yourself

I've always been a high achiever and sought to get results quickly. This has affected my ability to be patient even with myself. However, I have learnt that patience brings internal calm during external pressure. When it comes to purpose, I have learnt to think big, and when it comes to progress in my journey of faith; to celebrate small progress. Over the past several years of applying these principles, some changes were instant, for example, drinking and swearing. However, some of the coping mechanisms like pornography broke off over a period of time.

6. Set Small Goals

I used to view freedom and complete security in my identity as a destination. It was a place called 'there' and I'd be constantly striving to get 'there'. Although, God has an expected end I've learnt that freedom and security are in the daily decisions that we make rather than just the destination that we reach. Our ultimate goal is to be like Christ but that had to be broken up into small day-to-day decisions which stopped me from being pre-occupied with arriving and focusing on making effective daily choices.

7. Rediscover the Truth About God Has Said

My overall goal was to rediscover who God has made me to be and I did this through taking time daily to look through the Bible, Christian literature, edifying Christian messages and being around edifying friendships and relationships that built me up rather than tore me down.

8. Create New Habits, Self-Affirmations

Because of trust issues I wouldn't spend that much time with friends but as God was breaking the strongholds, I became more intentional with building friendships and activities that developed my calling. I was more conscious of limiting beliefs and wrote out Bible-based affirmations that built me up.

9. Forgive Yourself and Those Who Have Hurt You

Because I've accepted God's forgiveness it would be hypocritical not to forgive myself and those who have offended me. They may not have deserved my forgiveness, but God forgave me even when I didn't deserve it. I started to apply the principle of undeserved forgiveness not just to other people but to myself as well. Many of us are quick to forgive others but not willing to forgive ourselves. Although He is perfect, some of us need to forgive God for offences we've held towards Him. For example, some people have blamed God for the abuse that they suffered in childhood.

CHAPTER 6 SUMMARY

1. Through Jesus we have been given authority to confront and overcome the enemy and all trauma we have experienced.

2. We can use the principles of the Gospel to confront the 3 areas of our identity (belonging, worthiness and effectiveness).

3. There are 3 key foundations to our identity/authority in Christ.

4. There are 9 practical steps to help overcome trauma.

5. Jesus has given us authority and we can express that authority through to binding and loosing. We can express this authority when we pray prayer.

Questions For Study & Reflection

1. List all the negative words that have affected your sense of (a) worthiness (b) belonging (c) effectiveness.

_____

_____

_____

_____

2. Find bible verses that affirm your (a) worthiness (b) belonging (c) effectiveness.

_____

_____

_____

_____

3. Prayerfully reject and renounce every negative experience listed, in Jesus' name, and thank God for His promises concerning your (a) worthiness (b) belonging (c) effectiveness.

_____

_____

_____

4. Write biblical supported statements of affirmation in your identity (a) worthiness (b) belonging (c) effectiveness.

5. Follow the 9–step guideline to support you in overcoming personal trauma or fear. Journal your progress and reflection in each section.

CHAPTER 7

LIFE ON THE ROCK

DISCIPLESHIP, DEFINITIONS AND DESTINY

Afterward, Simba takes over the kingship as rain begins to fall. He also makes Nala his queen. Later, with Pride Rock restored to its usual state, Rafiki presents Simba and Nala's newborn cub to the assembled animals, continuing the circle of life.

It is a profound thing that Simba defeated Scar and returned to Pride Rock to live on the rock. Likewise, we as believers must learn to live on the Rock – Jesus Christ. He is the One in who we must rely on to maintain our freedom and deliverance.

In this chapter we will focus on:
- The deity of Jesus Christ
- Principles on freedom
- Biblical principles on maintaining freedom

The Deity of Jesus Christ

The word 'deity' means divine being or god. Before we can live a life with Christ as our foundation (rock), we must recognise who He is and be secure in the fact that He is God. One of the names given to describe God in the Old Testament is The Rock (Deuteronomy 32:3-4). Christ affirms His identity when speaking to Peter (Matthew 16:16-18). Below are some attributes of Christ that affirm His identity as God the Son:
- Pre-existent (John 1:1-3,27;16:26-28)

Jesus Himself witnessed to the fact of His own pre-existence. He existed before He was born. He declared this to the religious leaders, but they were not ready to receive it (John 8:58).

- Self-existent (John 1:4; 5:21-26)

The Son is the source of life and He has the power to give eternal life to all who believe. He has the power of an endless life (Hebrews 7:16). Only God has this power, which further affirms Christ's deity.

- Omnipotent (Ephesians 3:9, 1 Corinthians 8:6)

Jesus the Son of God has all power. He is Almighty. He is the Creator and Sustainer of the universe and the worlds, both seen and unseen.

  - He has power in heaven (Matthew 28:18)
  - He has power on earth (Matthew 28:18)
  - He has power over all nature (Matthew 8:23-27)
  - He has power over all demonic spirits (Luke 4:35-41)
  - He has power over all angels (1 Peter 3:22, Ephesians 1:20-22)

- Omniscient (Revelation 2:23, Hebrews 4:12-13)

The Son of God is all knowing and therefore nothing is hidden from His sight. This affirms His deity.

- Omnipresent (John 3:13, Matthew 18:20)

The Son of God is everywhere and fills all things. Because of this, He is able to gather with His people wherever and whoever they meet in His name.

- Perfectly Holy (Luke 4:34, Acts 4:27-30)

The Son of God is the only perfectly holy person that has ever walked the face of the earth.

- Perfectly Righteous (Jeremiah 23:5-6, 1 Corinthians 1:30)

The Son of God is The Lord our Righteousness. Yahweh Tsidkenu, spoken of in Jeremiah 23:5-6. This title is only given and applicable to God.

- Perfectly Faithful (Revelation 1:5, Philippians 2:8)

The Son of God was perfectly faithful to the Father.

- Divine worship given to Him

The Son of God was worshiped by:
  - Angels (Hebrews 1:6, Revelation 5:12-14)
  - Men (Matthew 8:2, 15:26)
  - Demons
  - All creation (Revelation 5:13)
  - Honoured equally with the Father (John 5:23)

- Acknowledged by demons (Matthew 8:29)

The Son of God was recognised by the entire Satanic kingdom of darkness.

- Fulfilled 4 Old Testament Offices

The Son of God fulfilled the main 4 Old Testament offices:
1. The Judge
2. The Priest
3. The Prophet
4. The King

Key Principles of Freedom

'Stand fast therefore in the liberty by which Christ has made us free, and do not be entangled again with a yoke of bondage.'
Galatians 5:1

The word liberty comes from eluthero which means 'to *liberate*, that is, (figuratively) to *exempt* (from moral, ceremonial or mortal liability) - deliver, make free'. The scripture above is very key in understanding biblical principles that relate to our liberty in Christ. There are some particular points in the verse above that we should pay close attention to in order to understand the biblical principles of walking in freedom through Christ.

- 'Stand fast' - Paul instructs the believers to take action. The term 'stand fast' implies that the individual is taking active and intentional steps to hold a position. This also indicates that although the work of freedom is achieved by God, the believer needs to take active participation with God in order to maintain alignment. Hebrews 2:1 also says 'Therefore we must give the more earnest heed to the things we have heard, lest we drift away'. Drift also means 'a continuous slow movement from one place to another'. Just like with any relationship, there is a mutual role each person plays to help sustain it. Although God does the majority, we have a responsibility to participate with Him (Philippians 2:12-13). 1 Timothy 4:12 also admonishes believers to 'fight the good fight of faith'. This indicates that salvation is free, but maintaining faith and freedom requires us to fight.

- 'Do not be entangled again' - Paul wrote to the people in Galatia to explain what it means to be justified through faith in Christ and the difference between Judaism and Christianity. After preaching The Gospel, the people experienced true liberty in Christ, however there were ministers who came to Galatia and 'added' to the Gospel that Paul preached and brought the believers back into a state of bondage.

How To Maintain Identity/Freedom

'Flee also youthful lusts; but pursue righteousness, faith, love, peace with those who call on the Lord out of a pure heart.'
2 Timothy 2:22

Within the verse above we can take 3 significant principles that encompass maintaining our liberty in Christ and freedom from past traumas.

1. Run From: 'Flee also youthful lusts'. The word 'flee' means to 'run away from a place or situation of danger'. We can only run from that which we perceive to be a threat or dangerous to our faith, healing and identity. Here lies the weapon of the enemy - deception. Oftentimes we can be deceived by the enemy to think that the thing that is most harmful to us is harmless. In order to sustain our freedom and identity, God's word highlights the things that can seriously damage our confidence with God. We must be humble enough to know that there are some enemies we fight simply by running from (see Joseph in Genesis 39:11-15). Although the verse above speaks specifically about fleeing lusts, the principle of departing from that which will damage you stands. Negative conversations, toxic relationships and destructive self-talk are all things we can 'flee' from. In summary, the believer is required to remove themselves from situations, actions, people and attitudes that can be damaging to their faith. We must ask God for true discernment to perceive the above with His perspective in order to truly identity a threat to flee from (1 Thessalonians 5:22, Psalm 1). An example of the 'run from' principle can be seen in the exodus of the Israelites from Egypt (See Exodus 12-19). God promised Israel freedom from their Egyptian oppressors, but the people were required to leave the environment, people and mentality that was keeping them captive. If you are going to walk in freedom, settle in your heart that you may need to change location, association and perspective.

2. Run to: 'pursue righteousness, faith, love, peace'. The second key point is the 'run to' or 'seek' principle. The definition of pursue is 'to follow or chase someone or something'. Although it is true that we are required to

run from evil to maintain freedom, this is not complete. Pursuit deals with priority, focus and engagement. When we pursue things that affirm our freedom and enhance our identity, we are automatically fleeing from things that can ensnare us. It is possible to flee and not pursue but it impossible to pursue and flee at the same time (Amos 5:5, Matthew 6:33).

3. Run with: 'with those who call on the Lord out of a pure heart'. Although we are instructed to turn from and run to, we were not created to do this by ourselves. Sometimes the believer may grow weary in the fleeing and pursuing and thus God has designed the church to promote and protect our liberty. There are 5 benefits of this:
   1. Discipleship - Discipleship is one of the greatest blessings the church can provide. Having a mentor and guide will help bring direction, understanding and journey.
   2. Accountability - We need others to support us in being accountable for who we are and who we are not.
   3. Community - Fellowship defined is 'friendly association, especially with people who share one's interests'. Fellowship itself is a gift that God gives to build relationship, transfer joy and protect our freedom. Some ignore this principle and suffer the consequences, however God created us to be relational beings.
   4. Correction - Correction is necessary for those who want to walk in continued freedom. Correction will bless the wise but be a curse to a foolish person. Correction helps you to make necessary adjustments to your identity that you may not have seen.
   5. Counsel - Counsel in direction, instruction and guidance. This is given from leaders, friends and pastors. However, you may need to seek

professional counselling depending on your issue.

MY STORY

What's brought deliverance in my life and helped me to maintain freedom has been to understand Christ's identity. Christ's identity is the basis and framework for my identity. One thing I have learnt is that I could never really build my identity until He began to reveal to me who He is. Knowing who Jesus is helped established what my rights are as a child of God.

Knowing who Jesus is also taught me principles of how I could walk in freedom. I realise that my identity in Christ is my greatest asset. My identity in Christ gives me authority to live in freedom. I've learnt that we don't fight for freedom alone, we fight from freedom. What I mean by this is that just like Adam was deceived into thinking he needed to get something he already had, the devil had deceived me in thinking I needed to obtain something I'd already received through Jesus. This is often his strategy with most people. He tried to use my addictions, my injuries, rejections, pornography etc. to tell me lies about who I am and make me think I had to perform in order to be free and accepted by God.

After failing miserably in my attempt to walk with God and be free in my own strength, relying on what Christ has done was my source of true freedom and security. I had to make a stand, but not by standing in my strength, by kneeling in His strength. I've realised that as we mature in our identity, we become more reliant on God. 2 Timothy 2:22 became such a real scripture for me in the journey of walking in my God-given identity.

Run From

Just like Simba had to run from some things to walk in his identity, I've had to, and still have to, run from some things to stand in my identity. I've learnt that if I am going to walk in God's identity I've had to and have to run from some mindsets, people and habits. I listed the names of everyone I had been intimate with and repented and broke soul ties with prayer. What was crazy about this, during the period of doing this the very people I prayed out were trying to come back into my life. Prayer alone was not enough. I needed to communicate my boundaries and enforce them. This was difficult and took a lot of courage because I was used to pleasing people at the expense of my own welfare. However, after the first few times it became easier. I used this same principle with friends, and it was as if over a couple of years, I went through major relationship changes. It is interesting because not all of my friends were bad, however, they weren't all beneficial for me.

There are 3 'A's that I learnt that strengthen addictive behaviours:
- Anonymity (when it is secret)
- Availability (easily accessible)
- Affordability (free or cheap)

After surrendering this area to Christ, I used the availability principle to block numbers on my phone and censor my internet usage. The difference this has made in walking in my identity and maintaining my freedom is as clear as night and day.

Run To

Although I had set these measures in place, the reality of my freedom, security in my identity and satisfaction in my life came solely from pursuing Christ. There are some that say in the 21st century 'we don't need to pursue God anymore', however, spending time with God has brought so much transformation in my life. Sometimes people get confused or frustrated with the term 'seeking God' and do not know what it looks like practically but there are several things that The Bible highlights about what it means to 'seek God', which I applied.

Meditation

One of the simplest ways we can 'run to God' is by thinking of Him. I think about God all the time and I'm sure that most believers do. The issue is that many believers don't think that this is a form of prayer or communing with God. In the morning, I have quiet time but throughout the day, I think things through with God and I think my prayers. When I'm in the shower, in the car, with friends, at work, doing hobbies, listening to music etc. Understanding this has helped me appreciate 1 Thessalonians 5:17 'pray without ceasing'.

When I saw the scripture 'pray without ceasing', I used to think it was impossible until I understood that we can have inward fellowship with God 24/7 through meditation.

Sincere Prayer

Some of my biggest frustrations in prayer were based on HOW to pray rather than WHO I'm praying to. I've always believed in Jesus, however, when I was a new believer, I had heard so many different methods to approach God in prayer it got both confusing and frustrating. What changed for me was understanding the importance of sincerity and identity in prayer. When it comes to sincerity, sometimes we tell God the things we think He wants to hear when in actual fact, God wants us to bring our heart and its contents to Him. Using the scriptures and being honest with God brought a lot of breakthrough. When it comes to identity, Jesus said, 'pray in this way, Our Father...'. Knowing that God is my Father, He loves me and wants to connect with me gives me confidence to approach Him and relate with Him in the context He has given me: Father.

Reading and Studying

One way to run to God is simply by reading about Him. Primarily, this involves the bible and other literature that affirms the bible.

Pursuing My Calling and Purpose

Pursuing my calling and God's purpose for my life has also been a key part of walking in freedom. After accepting my identity, I have to act out my identity. This involves acting out different truths that I've read in the Bible.

Calling: Calling is a strong inner conviction towards a particular way of life, career or vocation.

Purpose: Purpose is the original intent that God has for His creation.

My original passion was to play football, but when I got saved, I started serving in the ushering team. As I served, people began to recognise my gift of encouraging people, I was made a sound technician and then a youth pastor. Although pursuing this was challenging because of insecurities, doubts and inferiority complex; God used the pursuit of my purpose and calling to help me find more of my identity. You may not be called to be a pastor as well, but God has a purpose and calling for every single person. As you take steps to pursue that you will grow in your God-given identity.

Some of the practical things I did were:
- Bring solutions to problems I'm passionate about solving
- Use my gifts and skills
- Take risks and not be afraid to make mistakes

Run With

Although running to God brings a lot of freedom and confidence in our identity, we can get weary, frustrated and discouraged and NEED people to help us on our journey. One of the greatest weapons that God gives us in the journey of freedom is a godly friend. I was privileged to have a good friend who helped keep me accountable in living out my God-given identity. We'd catch up every other Monday on how we'd been 'running to' and 'running from'.

It was difficult at first because I was not used to that level of transparency and at times we clashed because I thought it was intrusive, however, the friendship taught me the power of vulnerability, communication, transparency and support. Our friendship has lasted over 10 years and I wouldn't have been able to overcome certain hurdles in my life without it.

Ultimately, our identity and freedom are rooted in Jesus Christ. The Lion King story serves as a great allegory that depicts the different stages of a believer's journey in Christ. Although your journey and my journey may differ, the principles that I'm sharing in this book should equip you to walk in your God-given identity and maintain freedom. My prayer for you is that just as God healed my scars and broke the lies that kept me bound, He will heal yours, break the limiting beliefs in your life and establish you to walk in all that God has made you to be, in Jesus' name. Amen.

CHAPTER 7 SUMMARY

1. We must recognise the identity of Jesus Christ in order to live our lives securely in Him.

2. There are several attributes of Jesus Christ in scripture that affirm His identity as God the Son.

3. God wants us to live free in Christ.

4. There are 3 principles in 2 Timothy 2:22 that help us to maintain our freedom in Christ: (1) Run from sin (2) Run to God (3) Run with godly people.

Questions For Study & Reflection

1. Memorise 2 Timothy 2:22.

   _____

   _____

   _____

   _____

2. List thoughts, places or things you need to run from. What practical steps can you take to do this?

   _____

   _____

   _____

   _____

3. List thoughts, places or things you need to run to. What practical steps can you take to do this?

   _____

   _____

   _____

   _____

4. List positive people you need to run with. What practical steps can you take to do this?

_____

_____

_____

_____

5. What practical steps can you take to pursue your identity and purpose?

_____

_____

_____

_____

END NOTE

COMMIT TO PROGRESS

The journey of identity is about becoming and not merely arriving. For the Christian, commit to growing daily and be willing to confront your fears in order to become all that God made you to be. For the non-Christian, your journey of identity truly begins when you repent from sin and put your faith in Jesus Christ. This begins the greatest adventure of faith you could imagine. My ultimate message to you is trust in God and watch how He works in you and through you to fulfil His promises. Identity must be founded in Christ and develops the more you are intentional with your relationship with Him. Fear and crisis will not hold you back, in Jesus' name. Amen.

AFFIRMATIONS

I AM CHOSEN BY GOD

I AM LOVED

I AM FORGIVEN

GOD IS MY FATHER

I AM BLESSED

GOD IS MY HEALER

GOD WILL KEEP ME IN PERFECT PEACE

I FIND JOY IN GOD'S MERCY

GOD WILL GUIDE ME FOREVER

MY PAST DOES NOT DEFINE ME

I AM ACCEPTED BY GOD

I AM WORTHY OF LOVE AND RESPECT

PRAYERS FOR SELF DELIVERANCE

FEAR
I loose myself from all fears, including fears from my childhood, fear from failures, fear from trauma, inherited fears from family and fear of success in Jesus Name.

REJECTION
I loose myself from all rejection, including rejection from family, friends, children, parents, partners, in-laws, professional rejection from colleagues, church rejection and self-rejection in Jesus name. I declare that I am unconditionally loved, completely forgiven and totally accepted by God in Jesus name.

SEXUAL SIN
I loose myself from all lust including pornography, masturbation, fornication, homosexuality, incest, beastiality, peodophilia, fantasy, soul ties and uncontrollable sexual urges.

UNGODLY SOUL TIES
I separation myself from **[mention the person's name],** emotionally, physically and spiritually. Whatever I gave you, I take it back and whatever you gave to me I give it back in the name of Jesus.
(Repeat prayer for every individual)

WITCHCRAFT
Father I loose myself from all involvement with witchcraft, the occult, all sorcery, rebellion, death, sickness, black magic, divination, channelling, ouija boards and palm reading in Jesus name.

UNFORGIVENESS

I loose myself from all sadness, unforgiveness, bitterness, depression, self pity, hatred, anger, resentment towards God, resentment towards **[mention the name of person]**. I forgive myself for my past mistakes and accept forgiveness from God in Jesus name.

ADDICTION

I loose myself from alcohol addiction, drug addiction, gluttony, nicotine, pornography, masturbation, self harm and all addictions in Jesus name.

RELIGION

I loose myself from all religious spirit, legalism, Jezebel spirit, intimidation, offence towards God and leadership, pride, cultism, church hurt, failure, performance based relationships and isolation in Jesus name.

THE MIND

I loose myself from all double-mindedness, confusion, insanity, past hurts, passivity, negative thinking, mental blocks, torment and worries in Jesus name.

CULTURE

I loose myself from all forms of racism, sexism, prejudice, ignorance, self-centredness and elitism in Jesus name.

REFERENCES

Conner, K., 1980. *Foundations of Christian doctrine*. Portland, Or.: Bible Temple Publications.

https://health.clevelandclinic.org/what-happens-to-your-body-during-the-fight-or-flight-response/

Oxford Language Dictionary [online]

ABOUT THE AUTHOR

Emmanuel Adeseko is an apostolic voice, leader, businessman and experienced social worker. A phenomenal communicator of the Gospel and a prolific voice; he writes to teach, edify and transform. Emmanuel Adeseko has been in ministry since the age of 15 and founded New Covenant Ministries in September 2017, based in Birmingham, England.

For enquires & bookings:
EmmanuelAdeseko@hotmail.co.uk
Instagram: Emmanuel Adeseko
Website: www.emmanueladeseko.co.uk

Printed in Great Britain
by Amazon

39792560R00066